WHORL AND WHEEL

THE STORY OF HANDSPINNING IN SCOTLAND
BY
SU GRIERSON

Contents

Introduction

No one can say how far back in time the Scots people began to make cloth by spinning either animal or vegetable fibres. However, the artifacts of spinning, the whorls and wheels that are most commonly seen in museums and private collections today, relate mainly to the last 400 years and that is the time span this booklet will be concerned with.

To understand the story of handspinning it is necessary to see more than just the tools of the craft. The purpose of spinning in the first place was to produce textiles, and these in turn related strongly to the raw materials used. Economics, governmental policy and even climate dictated the availability of these.

The design of spinning tools was partly determined by each particular maker and partly by functional necessity; many styles will be illustrated and described in the coming pages.

Because spinning was essentially a domestic industry right up to the time of mechanisation, many of the finest examples of spinning wheels are still to be found in the homes of the descendants of the original owners. For several generations wheels were unfortunately being "put out" because, to many, they symbolised the hardship and poverty of earlier times. Today distance has broken those hard memories and it is now a different story. Wheels are taken down from the attic, dusted off and polished. It is sometimes really surprising to see the way in which wheels are cherished as an important link with the past by those who have not the faintest idea of how they work or of the traditions that go with them. It is to be hoped that this little book will go some way towards introducing "The story of handspinning in Scotland".

In Scotland the two fibres traditionally employed for spinning were flax and wool. They differ from each other so widely in terms of cultivation and use that they have to be considered quite separately.

PLATE 1. Wooden spindle shaft with separate stone whorl or "make-weight".

1

Sheep and Wool

The earliest type of sheep in Scotland were probably very similar to the small Soay sheep. This breed still thrives in Scotland today due to its survival as a feral flock on the island of Soay in the remote St Kilda Islands. These lie in the Atlantic Ocean 110 miles west of the Scottish mainland. There are records of wild sheep being on St Kilda in the 14th century, although they are thought to be the product of early domestication rather than truly wild. Their behaviour, however, is certainly very wild indeed! As most handlers of Soays will agree, it is a very intelligent, agile and speedy animal with a dedicated commitment to not being handled or herded. Its unnerving habit of facing its would-be captors and then running straight towards them leaping and jinking at the last moment to avoid capture has caused more than one shepherd's dog to admit defeat and retreat for home with its tail between its legs. Reports exist of some wild chases taking place on St Kilda each year with many sheep going over the cliffs to their death. In later years when meat rather than wool was required the islanders apparently preferred the less hazardous method of stalking the sheep with guns!

The Soay fleece is soft, short and very dense. It does not require shearing but it is rather plucked off the sheep, a practice known as 'rooing'. Each year in early summer the new season's growth of wool begins, and as it reaches a few millimetres in length a break point occurs between it, and the old wool from the previous year. This in turn allows the old wool to be peeled off without any undue pressure being applied and with no discomfort to the animal. Indeed some appear to relax and enjoy it, whilst others twitch a little as if they are being tickled.

PLATE 2. Small, horned, Soay sheep, originally from the St Kilda Islands.

The animals of a flock do not all get the new rise at the same time and indeed it does not naturally occur uniformly over the whole body. In St Kilda in recent times the stubborn patches i.e. those where the break had not occurred, were eased away with a knife.

Soay wool is normally mid-brown although about one third of feral flocks will be a paler biscuit colour. Some animals also have a longer hairy coat.

It is thought that the white sheep introduced to Scotland by the Romans probably crossed with the native breeds and eventually produced a new Scottish type that came to be known as either the "Dunface" or the "Old Scottish Shortwool". Hairy 'muirland' sheep were also known to exist and from the melting-pot of these variously coloured animals there evolved fine wooled breeds such as those in Shetland, and coarser wooled breeds like the seaweed-eating sheep of North Ronaldsay.

Because of the great amount of woodland that covered Scotland until well into the 17th century, sheep were kept in small family owned flocks that probably contained a variety of wool type and colour. It is further very likely that some selective breeding took place in favour of white animals due to the importance of the need for fleece that would spin and dye well.

The Black Book of Taymouth which is an account, started in 1598, of the affairs of the Campbells of Glenurchy, records a sheep clip at the East End of Loch Tay in 1605. The total weight of white wool was 7 'stanis' and 2 'qrs' and of black wool 2 'stanis' and 1 'pund'. Of this clip 2 'stanis' of white wool was given to the laird's daughter Margaret Campbell, and also to a Christine Doig for making the laird's clothes. This amounted to one quarter of the whole white wool clip. Quite obviously this flock was not of economic significance to the owners but simply provided the estate with wool, meat and most probably also milk and butter.

It was at the end of the 18th century that Scotland suffered the enormous social, agricultural and ecological impact of the introduction of two new sheep breeds. Firstly the Cheviots came into the lowlands, and then both the Black-face and Cheviot breeds were brought to the Highlands. Throughout Scotland native flocks were being 'improved' and from the writings and journals of travellers in Scotland at that time it can be seen that a tremendous diversity of sheep, and consequently wool types, existed in various parts of the country. This in turn greatly affected the art and the end product of the spinner.

The wool of Galloway had a long-standing tradition of high quality, but the local people had not always the skill to spin and weave it well. The Isle of Oronsay was another place producing excellent wool which was said to be long, fine and snow-white. Apparently the Oronsay sheep had originally come from Ireland, but on other Hebridean islands the sheep were still aboriginal and unimproved. It seemed that the breed on South Uist differed from anywhere else having 4, 6 or 8 horns and indifferent wool. These might well have been similar to the Jacob sheep currently enjoying a revival in Britain.

At the end of the 18th century the sheep of Shetland were known to possess the ancient characteristic of a two-layer fleece. In this case an outer layer of long coarse hair-like fibres covers an undercoat of short fine soft wool. The Highland Society report on Shetland sheep made in 1790 says that when the sheep were plucked in early summer the longer hairs did not come away with the bulk of the fleece, but stayed on the animal and were eventually moulted in the autumn.

This feature of a double-layer fleece could account for a comment made in 1705 by John Spreull, a prolific writer on Scottish affairs of that time, who complained of the poor quality of Scottish wool, saying that the "hairie part spoils the fyner".

The sheep of Orkney had clearly developed their own characteristics by the late 18th century. Writing of that time, John Firth in his book about Orkney records that the sheep there were known by the delightful name of "bussie broos" on account of the tuft of wool that formed a kind of forelock on the brow. He also lists the colours of these animals as being grey, tawny, brown, black or white. They were small sheep that roamed at large on the islands and were always rooed rather than shorn.

These accounts and many more like them indicate the complexity of Scottish sheep and wool types during the 17th and 18th centuries.

Smearing

It might be thought that the great diversity of wool types would have caused Scottish spinners enough problems, but there was a far greater hazard to craftsmanship and it was caused by the practice of sheep smearing.

The modern system of dipping sheep to control parasites and prevent diseases such as sheep scab did not begin until 1850. Prior to that, the only known method of control was to cover the sheep with a mixture of tar oil and melted butter.

Normally 14lbs of butter, usually made from sheep's milk, was melted with 1 gall. of tar, and it is said that a man could smear 35 sheep in a day. Other mixtures recorded are, pine tar and brown grease, spirits of tar and whale oil, and tobacco juice and soap with tar.

Needless to say, before the wool could be spun, a great deal of scouring (washing) and preparation had to be done. Whilst not every sheep was tarred, those that were not also presented a problem since the contamination from parasites and the inevitable scratching they caused clearly created poor fleeces.

In 1770 wool from the Highlands was reported to suffer a loss of 50% in the scouring and if it had been tarred then 62% was said to be lost. Since the average fleece weight of this time has been estimated at only 1.5 lb., obtaining good wool for spinning was clearly not an easy task.

Scouring was generally done with urine and water and possibly alkaline plant or seaweed ashes. But the dirty wool did not go to waste. In a booklet written for housewives in 1676, the author Gervase Markham, instructed them to cut out and save all the tarred locks, pitch feltings etc, and make them into coarse coverlets. What a task!

Oiling

After all the previous difficulties had been overcome, the spinner would eventually find herself with some clean washed wool ready for use, and she had then to tease and card or comb it before she could begin. Carding and combing are explained on page 6 but here we will deal with another problem she had to face. After the fairly vigorous scouring to which it had been subjected, the wool would have been dry and brittle and impossible to spin into a smooth strong yarn for weaving. This meant that she had firstly to oil the wool in order to replace the lost lanoline.

Modern day spinners use sweet smelling baby oil or refined olive oil, but what was available in the 17th and 18th centuries? References have been found to the use of a very wide range of substances but which one was used by each spinner depended, no doubt, on what was locally available at the time. The choice included the following items — unsalted butter, fish liver oil, whale oil, whale oil and tar melted together, tallow made from sheep's fat, lard, butter from ewe's milk, rape oil, clarified goose grease, swine's grease, olive oil, fulmar oil, the worst sort of butter and the juice expressed from the root of common fern.

We can certainly believe John Firth in Orkney who said that this process of oiling made the cloth dark in colour and smelly, but he assures us that after weaving, the cloth was washed with soap and soda.

Once again Gervase Markham gave his housewives clear instructions on the application of the oil which he said should be applied after the wool was dyed and before being spun. The wool, he told them, should be teased and laid in a flat round bed, then oiled, mixed and turned over for a further application. He also cautioned that if too much oil was used, the wool would not draw during spinning but would fall apart, so a little should be put on at first and the wool tried on the wheel as a test. Three pounds of grease or oil, he said, was sufficient for ten pounds of wool.

PLATE 3. Tools of the trade. Back from l. to r. Flax heckle, Pair of hand cards, Niddy-Noddy. Front. 3 drop spindles.

Carding and Combing

In order to achieve an evenly spun yarn, wool needs to be either combed, which leaves the fibres lying in their natural growing position but free from any matting and lumps (see Plate no. 4), or can be carded, which breaks up the natural locks and creates a sausage-like "rolag" of fibres (see Plate no. 5).

Combed wool, with all the fibres lying parallel, was spun into smooth firm yarns described as "worsted"; whilst carded fleece was spun into a bulkier yarn termed "woollen".

PLATE 4. Combing produces a continuous 'roving' of straight fibres.

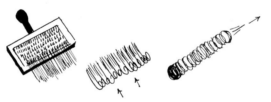

PLATE 5. After carding, wool fibres are rolled into a 'rolag'.

Carders with metal teeth were known to have been made in France since the 13th century, but no evidence exists to indicate that they were manufactured at an early date in Scotland. Perhaps the most interesting Scottish reference to both combs and cards is to be found in the Black Book of Taymouth, where in an inventory made in 1600 of the "woman hous" at Finlarg we find that there were 4 pairs of old 'stok cardis' and two pairs of wool combs described as 'woll kamis'. So clearly, by 1600, both wool combs and cards were in use. Evidence to support the idea that these items were imported is found in a list of the goods being carried on a ship seized in 1349 whilst on its way to Scotland. Wool carding combs were one item in a cargo of amazing diversity.

From various references it seems most likely that coarse blankets were made from wool that had only been teased prior to spinning. Combs were used to prepare both flax and also the long stapled wool fibres that were spun as lustrous worsteds for the close weaving used in the traditional hard tartan. Carding was used mostly for making softer weft and knitting yarns spun from short stapled woolly fleece.

Spindles

The earliest tool employed for putting a twist into thread was the spindle. This is true not only of Scotland but of all cultures worldwide.

A spindle requires a weight sufficient to create momentum when given an initial twirl, and it needs a stick to which the yarn is attached and around which the spun yarn can be wound. The spindles illustrated in Plate no. 3 show the two main types used in Scotland. The first is simply a tapered length of wood or bone used with the thick end downward to create the necessary weight. The longest spindle of this type to be recorded was 14¾ ins. Sometimes spindles of this type were embellished with a little decorative carving.

A more sophisticated variety of spindle was made by passing a straight stick through the centre of a whorl which was usually fashioned from stone although sometimes wood or bone was used. In some instances the whorl was permanently attached to the stick but in others this "make-weight" could be removed once the ball of wound-on yarn was heavy enough to provide the momentum. A further type of spindle used in some areas in the 19th century employed the same basic principle as that of the whorl and stick, but was made from a potato preserved in glycerine. Although less permanent, it would have been more easily made and replaced.

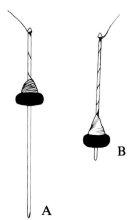

PLATE 6. Two spindles. A. Spindle with long shaft for thigh rolling. B. Drop spindle.

Whichever style of spindle was used there was always a notch in the upper end of the stick so that the yarn could be secured there during spinning by means of a simple slip knot.

It seems that in Scotland there were two main techniques employed for using the spindle. From a standing position the spindle was twirled by a firm twist with the fingers and was then left to hang freely as it twisted the yarn. It was also possible when standing to get the twist started by rolling the spindle shaft down the thigh, but this method is more suited to spinning in a sitting position. For this method the spindle must have a long shaft extending below the whorl. After the momentum is started along the thigh, the spindle is allowed to reach the floor and continue spinning there like a child's top.

Because the yarn is under greater tension when spun in the "free-fall" position it is likely to be a harder, more firmly twisted thread especially suited for use as a warp in weaving. For flax thread which needed to be spun even finer and harder than wool, heavier whorls were normally used. The softer yarn from a supported spindle was likely to be more suited to knitting or as a weft thread.

In Chambers Encyclopedia of 1895 there is a poem which well describes the use of a spindle from a seated position . . .

> *To save their plaiding coats some had*
> *upo the haunch a bonnet braid*
> *or an auld wecht or kairding skin*
> *to rub and gar the spindle rin*
> *down to the ground wi twirling speed*
> *an twine upo the floor the thread.*

Because of the use of stone whorls, spindles were frequently called "rocks", and fireside gatherings where the women gossiped and re-told local folk stories as they spun were called "rockings". In 1769 after a visit to Breadalbane, Thomas Pennant used the term when he wrote in his journal that the lord of the district gave annually among his people a large number of spinning wheels "which would soon cause the disuse of the rock".

When spindle spinning, the unspun fibre was normally held on a stick called a distaff. These sticks were tucked under the arm that was not involved with working the spindle. Distaffs varied from simple sticks with a notched end to intricately carved heirlooms often given as love tokens.

Before being attached to a distaff, the wool or flax had to be combed and tied as a loose bunch rather than carded.

Because of the mobility that this method of spinning allowed, it was often done at the same time as other chores. Pennant tells us that "the women spin with rocks which they do while they attend their cattle on the hills". But surely there were few who could rival the good lady in Orkney whom John Firth assures us could herd cattle, sing, dance, run backward and forward and produce yarn on a spindle at the same time!

It seems that whilst spindle spinning was still common-place in the Hebrides in 1850, by 1884 it had largely died out. Although some stalwart individuals were still practicing the craft well into this century, they were a very small minority.

PLATE 7. A painting depicting yarn being wound on to a pirn for the weavers shuttle. The skein is held on a revolving swift at the winders left hand side. (Photograph printed by Courtesy of Mr and Mrs Nigel Anderson, Perthshire).

PLATE 8. A beautiful 3 flyer wheel at Hill House, Helensburgh. (Photograph by F. W. Bradford Photography, Helensburgh. Printed by Courtesy of The National Trust for Scotland).

PLATE 9. An unusual style of wool wheel, with 'Boomerang' supports. (Photograph by B. S. Wilson, Museums Officer Orkney. Printed by Courtesy of Tankerness House Museum, Kirkwall).

PLATE 10. A typical Hebridean Wheel which was made on the now uninhabited island of Mingulay. This wheel is still owned by descendants of the original owner. (Photograph printed by Courtesy of Mrs Morag MacPherson, Perthshire).

The Muckle Wheel

The muckle or great wheel was a simple development from spindle spinning. By looking at Plate no. 11 it is easy to see that the spindle was just turned on its side and rotated by a band that encircled both the spindle and the large wheel.

Because of the difference in size between the very large wheel and the small whorl on on the spindle, every revolution made by the wheel would cause the spindle to turn many times. By being large and heavy the wheel, once set in motion, would continue to turn under its own momentum. This meant that one push from the hand would keep the spindle in rotation long enough for quite a long thread to be spun. Indeed, with the largest wheels, the spinner could walk backwards for some distance pulling out a thread before the rotation stopped (hence its other name "walking wheel").

When a length had been spun and the wheel slowed, then the spinner stepped forward and, whilst holding the thread at right angles to the spindle, slowly reversed the wheel to unwind the thread from the point of the spindle. Then, by slowly turning the wheel in the original clockwise direction, the spun yarn was wound onto the back of the spindle always leaving the point clear for further spinning.

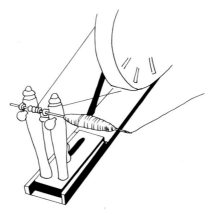

PLATE 11. Detail of the spindle head arrangement on the Muckle Wheel illustrated on the front cover.

When Gervase Markham instructed his housewives in the art of using "the great wooll wheel" he knowingly said that the "actions . . . must be got by practice not relation". He cautioned them to make their thread according to the nature of the wool rather than their own desire, and he further complained that the English housewife made no diversity of spinning and "spins every thread alike, whilst the more experienced make two kinds of thread one called weft and the other warp or woofe". Of course he did specify the English housewife and perhaps the Scots were more experienced at such things. It is certainly related that the women of Holland were very skilled at judging the amount of twist needed for any particular purpose.

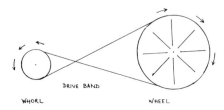

PLATE 12. *In order to ply yarns on a Muckle wheel (see 'ply', page 30), the rotation of the spindle can be reversed by crossing the drive band.*

The earliest muckle wheels had the spindles tied in place with plaits of straw which soon became smooth in use allowing very free rotation, but these were later replaced by leather bearings. There are no precise dates for the introduction of muckle wheels to Scotland, but the great amount of sea trade between the east coast ports of Scotland and the Dutch sea-ports might very well have led to the early purchase of a few European wheels prior to their general introduction.

In 1600 at Finlarg and Balloch, The Black Book of Taymouth recorded the existence of 2 spinning wheels, 2 new spinning wheels, 2 old spinning wheels and 2 wheel spindles. It is possible to assume from this that the items called wheel spindles were in fact muckle wheels and that the others were flyer wheels (see page 18), since it would otherwise seem strange to identify them differently. It could also be that wheel spindles were no more than spare spindles for the muckle wheel, but a further item on the list was 'iron spindles' which would seem to cover this. However, as there is no supportive evidence to suggest that flyer wheels existed in Scotland this early, it would be unwise to make a judgement based on this one interpretation. It certainly is clear though, that spinning wheels of some kind were being used in Scotland prior to 1600.

There are few surviving old muckle wheels in Scotland. This might very well be due to the fact that in Scotland, and particularly in the Highlands and Islands, spindle spinning continued well into the 18th century when flyer wheels and flax spinning became dominant. It is likely for this reason that spindles were directly supplanted by flyer wheels and that muckle wheels designed for wool spinning would have been used less in Scotland than in England and Wales where wool was more important than flax during the 18th century.

In the late 18th century records of Wm. Wilson & Son, a tartan weaving firm in Bannockburn, some tartans are referred to as "rock and wheel". From the context it is clear that this term refers to a quality of cloth rather than its pattern; and suggests the use of a tightly spun warp thread, as might have been made on the spindle or rock, with a softer wheel-spun weft. This was indeed a well known method of cloth construction, in parts of Europe, at a time when muckle wheels and spindles were in use at the same time.

Pirn Winders

Occasionally one comes across what appear to be very rustic muckle wheels, often small in size. These will almost certainly have been pirn winders used for loading yarn on to the weaver's shuttle.

No spinning was done on these wheels, but as can be seen in Plate no. 7 the prepared yarn was wound off a revolving swift directly on to the spindle. This would first have received a wrapping of skin that could be slipped off together with its yarn once loaded, or else the yarn was wound on to individual steel rods that could be removed and exchanged when full.

Wheels intended for use as winders frequently had raised sides on the table forming a box-like container to hold the completed pirns. They usually also had a small handle on the wheel to facilitate even turning with the right hand, whilst using the left to control the yarn.

The work of winding frequently fell to women and children, but sometimes a "retired" weaver such as the Dutch gentleman in the illustration on Plate no. 7 would be thus employed.

It should be said that it was perfectly possible to use a muckle wheel for the purpose of winding, but since winding for a weaver was a full time job, the wheel could not then have also been used for spinning.

Flax and Linen

The cultivated flax plant, Linum usitatissimum, likes ample rainfall and temperate climate during growth, so it is not difficult to understand why Scotland, and particularly the east coast were (and indeed still are) well suited to its production. The long straight and strong fibres within the stalk of the plant reach right down into the root, so that at harvest the plants had to be pulled from the ground rather than cut.

After pulling, the bundles of flax were beaten against a spiked rippling board that removed the seed which could in turn be used for making linseed. Although, if the primary purpose of the crop was to obtain seed, then a

PLATE 13. Flax. To gain longer fibres, flax seeds are planted very close together thus forcing the plants to grow taller.

different variety and cultivation method were needed. When the seeds had been removed the flax was stooked in the field until dry.

The next part of the process was retting, which in Scotland was usually achieved by immersion of the flax in boggy holes dug in specially selected sites. The smell from these holes was said to be appalling, but they served their purpose of creating a fermentation which destroyed the adhesive matter binding the fibres together. Because of the danger of over-retting, the process was often finished by laying the fibres out on the grass for a week or so.

The woody outer skins were removed next by some form of beating or beetling, after which the crop could move on to the next stage of preparation known as scutching. For this, the flax was held against a wooden scutching board and beaten with a wooden blade to start the process of separating out the individual fibres from the bundles in which they naturally lie. This separation was continued on metal combs called heckles which varied in size. For coarse fibre, combs with widely spaced teeth were used, but fine quality flax would start on these and then progress down to combs with very closely set teeth.

Throughout this process much wastage occurred of coarse and broken fibres, but this "tow" was made into ropes or very coarse sack-like cloth.

Linen has been a domestic product of Scotland from ancient times. Linen weaving was well established in the 15th century and there are many references to the ancient Scots wearing linen shirts. It has been calculated that in 1663, 1200 people were employed in the Scottish linen trade. Indeed the spinning by spindle and, to a lesser extent, muckle wheel that have already been discussed with regard to wool spinning would also have applied to the use of home grown flax. However, the flax and linen industry expanded so dramatically during the 18th century that it seems most relevant to discuss flax in terms of these later developments.

In 1727, a body was constituted that was called "The Commissioners and Trustees for improving Fisheries and Manufacturing in Scotland". Although

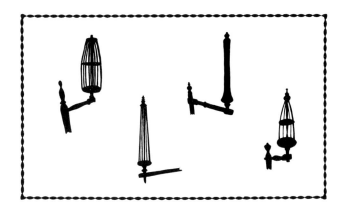

PLATE 14. A selection of distaff styles. Although rare, a few interesting and beautiful 18th and 19th Century examples can still be seen in museum collections.

hardly knowing where to turn in their effort to put Scotland's dismal affairs to rights, one of their decisions was to develop the flax industry.

At first they met with little response from the public, but after some tempting bounties had been offered by the government for those growing flax, the idea seemed to catch on! Between 1727 and 1748 the amount of flax grown in Scotland trebled. It soon became apparent however that this was being grown mostly in the already efficient arable regions with very little in the Highlands and Islands.

It was only after the Jacobite uprising of 1745, when estates were forfeited to the Crown and an act of parliament in 1753 established the need for "civilising and improving" the Highlands, that serious attempts were made to establish flax growing in that part of Scotland.

At the outset the "Trustees of the Forfeited Estates" were given £3,000 per annum for 9 years to promote the growing and cultivation of flax in the Highlands. They responded by establishing spinning schools, and also by sponsoring skilled flax raisers, hecklers and weavers to move from the cities into remote areas. They gave free wheels to those who could spin, and flax seed was sent free or at a nominal cost in the first instance to get flax growing started. In a genuine and desperate attempt to provide work and prosperity for the people of the Highlands, money was poured into this project. Although some areas did prosper as a result of the introduction of flax, notably the Orkney Islands, in general flax did not prove to be the salvation of the Highlands.

It certainly is true to say, however, that as a direct result of the flax era the traditions and skills of the spinner were reborn.

15

Flax Spinning

The spinning of flax made a considerable impact on the everyday life of the people. It was intended, somewhat optimistically by the government, that each district should have teachers and spinning instructors, and although this never happened on the intended scale, some districts certainly did benefit from the scheme. We know, for example, that at about 1760 there was a school teacher at Rannoch by the name of Dougal Buchanan who taught reading, writing and catechism to the children, and catechism to their parents. His wife, who was a mistress of the art of spinning, instructed the tenants' wives and daughters to spin and sew, and the boys to knit stockings.

PLATE 15. A flax wheel with sloping or 'cocked-up' table. The distaff at one side could be rotated into a position convenient to the spinner.

As happened on the Argyll estate, flax raising and spinning was sometimes almost forced on tenants. Instructions given to the factor in 1792 said that on the island of Icolmkill (now known as Iona) much of the rent should henceforth be paid in linen yarn or cloth, as the island was well suited to raising flax and there were many idle women!

In other places the women were known to be very industrious indeed in their attention to their domestic duty of spinning. In 1618 Taylor (the water poet) wrote "and I am sure that in Scotland beyond Edinburgh I have been at houses like castles for building, the master of the house his beaver being his blue bonnet. One that will wear no other shirts but of the flaxe that growes on his own ground, and his wives, daughters and servants spinning, that hath his stockings, hose and jerkin of the wool of his own sheepes backes".

16

PLATE 16. Flax wheel with two flyers, a central distaff dressed with flax, and a water pot hanging from the distaff. The wheel is 'sunk' in the table.

An even clearer picture of this domestic industry is provided by George Penny. Writing in 1836, but referring to earlier times in Perthshire, he said "formerly great quantities of flax were brought to this market (Dunning). Farmers were then in the practice of keeping a number of maids, principally with a view to spinning. The produce of their labour forming the chief source from whence the rent was made up: a farmer's kitchen exhibiting in the long winter's evenings much of the bustle of a little manufactury: three or four maids spinning: the mistress of the house reeling their yarn, and the master, men servants and herd boys assiduously employing their vacant time in knitting mits and hose or occupied in reparing horse gear: while the whole party were edified by the interesting horrors of a ghost story". However, Penny goes on to say that at the time of writing "the great changes in the management of rural affairs, and the unwearying efforts of the giant steam having banished the cheery thrifty wheel from the ingle side, little flax is now grown in the country".

By 1895, Alexander Ross, writing about Scottish home industries, tells us that it was then a rare sight indeed to see a wife and her daughters sitting spinning by the cottage fire.

The full impact of home grown and hand spun flax lasted little more than a hundred years.

17

Flyer or "Saxony" Wheels

It is frequently written that flyer wheels reached Scotland from Holland "by 1700". As has been discussed already in the section on muckle wheels, there is a real possibility that at least some individual wheels arrived very much before that time. Certainly what was known as the "Dutch" wheel was taken to Ireland in the middle of the 17th century. There are suggestions that some wheels came to the Highlands from Ireland, although the legality of the enterprise is usually questioned!

The feature that made the saxony wheel so overwhelmingly successful was initially a flyer which offered a continuous wind-on of yarn on to a removable and free moving bobbin. And later the introduction of a treadle to gain continuous momentum of the wheel.

How the Flyer Wheel Works

Plate no. 19 shows the progression of yarn, firstly through the orifice then around a hook on the flyer arm which guides it on to the bobbin. As each section of bobbin fills, the yarn is moved to the next hook and so on until all is filled.

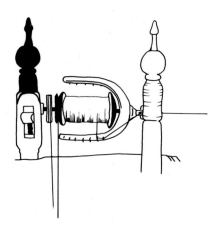

PLATE 17. Typical 'flyer' arrangement, with whorl and bobbin being driven by one continuous but doubled drive-band. The left hand 'maiden' can be rotated to raise or lower the end of the flyer thus altering the drive-band tension.

The yarn is pulled in to the flyer by virtue of the fact that the flyer and bobbin are rotating at different speeds. Plate no. 18 shows that the bobbin not only rotates independently from the flyer but that it has a groove at one end. The whorl can be seen to have two grooves at different depths. The bobbin groove is always deeper than either of the whorl grooves.

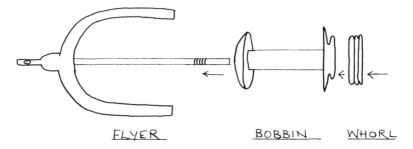

FLYER   BOBBIN   WHORL

PLATE 18. Method of assembling flyer, bobbin and whorl. The whorl is screwed tight onto the shaft.

There are two main methods of using these grooves to obtain different turning speeds for flyer and bobbin.

The flyer is rotated by a driving band going around the outside rim of the wheel and also around one of the grooves in the whorl. Each time the wheel rotates once, the whorl and flyer will rotate many times. The exact number of times is determined by the ratio of the wheel circumference to the circumference of the whorl groove being used. (The deeper groove will cause more rotations than the shallower).

PLATE 19. During spinning the yarn passes through the flyer orifice, around the guide hooks and on to the bobbin.

Plate no. 17 shows how a long, continuous but doubled driving band passes not only around the whorl as just described, but also around the groove of the bobbin. Since this groove is deeper than either of the grooves on the whorl, the bobbin will be driven at a faster speed than the flyer. Because it is moving at greater speed, the bobbin will pull yarn in and automatically wrap it around itself.

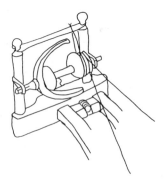

PLATE 20. The head of a 'boomerang' style wheel with a brake-band tied to a top bar.

The other method of obtaining two speeds is by slowing down the speed of the bobbin (which if it was not driven by a band but was left to its own devices would be carried around at the same speed as the flyer). In this case the flyer will be travelling faster than the slowed down bobbin, and will wrap the yarn around the bobbin thus pulling in more yarn all the time.

Plate no. 20 shows how a braking system can be arranged to slow down the speed of the bobbin, by tying a friction band around the groove on the bobbin and onto a top bar built into the wheel for this purpose. This system is frequently called "scotch tension".

Although wheels were designed with variations of these principles, these are the two basic methods of making a spinning wheel "work".

Twist is put into yarn before and/or during its progress on to the bobbin. For each single revolution of the flyer, one twist is put in the yarn. The degree to which this twist is spread out along the yarn is dependent on the speed at which the yarn travels in to the bobbin.

Types of Flyer Wheel

By the end of the 18th century, flyer wheels could be found throughout Scotland. Certainly there were groups of people in more remote places who still spun with a spindle and distaff, but had they wished it they could almost certainly have obtained a wheel without too much difficulty.

Scotland had at that time literally hundreds of individual craftsmen making wheels, so it is not surprising that individual styles and designs should start to appear. It is so tempting to try and classify these into area or district styles, or to suggest that certain styles were always related to specific types of spinning, but every rule devised can be rapidly shattered. The truth is that there were as many styles of wheel to spin on as there were chairs to sit on! However, these styles all related to two basic types of wheel.

During the 18th century, wheels were almost always defined as being either lint wheels (for flax), or wool wheels. This statement could be interpreted as indicating that flyer wheels were used for flax and muckle wheels for wool, indeed that is a common interpretation. However, in Scotland, this terminology was used in areas where there is direct evidence of the flyer wheel immediately replacing the spindle, and it seems most likely that different types of flyer wheel are being referred to. Since there is no distinction to be made between general styles of flyer wheels made for either wool or flax, one must look at detail to know which is which.

A lint wheel always had . . .

1. Small bobbins (the thread was very fine).
2. Small hooks on the flyer which were closely spaced.
3. A narrow orifice (to hold the fine thread steady during spinning).
4. A distaff.
5. A water receptacle or hollow in which to place a small bowl.

The water receptacle was an essential part of flax spinning as by keeping the fingers damp the spinner moistened the natural gummy substance in the fibre, and also smoothed down the fine tendrils that could otherwise create a hairy look to the finished yarn.

Since flax is spun into a fine thread with a high degree of twist, a high wheel/whorl size ratio is desirable. However, of the flax wheels that have been seen and measured, the ratios have usually, but not always, been higher than in wool wheels, so this can not be seen as an infallible guide.

Wool wheels generally have a larger flyer, bobbin and orifice, although no standard sizes can be given because to a certain extent they must relate to the size of the whole wheel. For wool spinning, no distaff or water pot are needed.

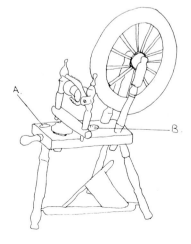

PLATE 21. This wheel was designed for flax, note A. hole to take a distaff, and B. hollow for water bowl.

Styles of Flyer Wheel

A selection of popular styles of Scottish wheel are illustrated below. They fall into two main categories, either those called "horizontal" where the flyer lies to the side of the wheel or those known as "vertical" where the wheel is normally below but occasionally above the flyer.

The very small vertical wheel is today often referred to as a Shetland style. It is recorded as being in those islands by about 1800 and was sometimes called a "spinnie". Whilst it certainly was a very popular style in Shetland, many islanders owned larger horizontal type wheels and also in more recent times some families preferred Scandinavian type wheels imported from Norway.

Horizontal wheels with a flat or slightly sloping table are similar to the "Dutch" wheel thought to be the first type imported by Scotland. It is a style which seems to have predominated in the Western Isles where it was particularly well suited for spinning the firm single-ply woollen yarn used in the weaving of Harris Tweed.

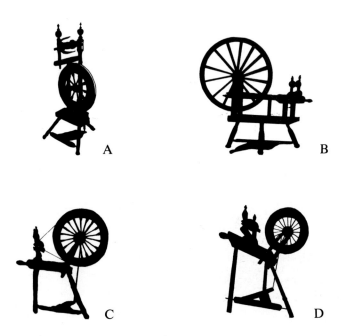

PLATE 22. A. Small vertical 'Shetland' style wheel. B. Large horizontal 'Scandinavian' style wheel. C. Hebridean wheel of solid construction. D. Delicate, horizontal wheel with sloping table.

A number of examples of wheels with two flyers can still be found in Scotland. Intended for spinning two threads, one with each hand, they were designed specifically for spinning flax and although it is feasible to spin long-stapled combed wool on such wheels, it is difficult and unlikely to have occurred to any extent. Certainly all references to two-handed spinning in Scotland relate to the use of flax, and the purpose was quite simply to increase the output of each spinner.

In her book "Spinning Wheels" Patricia Baines quotes as Englishman called Thomas Firmin who wrote in 1681 that children should be taught to spin firstly on a single flyer wheel where they should learn to become proficient at spinning with either hand, and only then should they progress to the double wheel. In all of the Scottish two-handed wheels examined, the two flyers were designed to be driven by one long doubled driving band passing over the top of both whorls.

For two-handed spinning it became necessary to have a distaff that could swing in to a central position where it was accessible to both flyers, rather than out to one side as is normal for single flyer wheels.

In the major flax-growing areas of Scotland, two-handed wheels were in general use by the end of the 18th century. Although of unknown date, the wheel seen in Plate no. 16 probably originated in Fife and is a classic example of a high quality flax wheel.

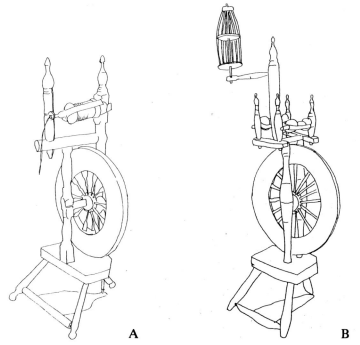

PLATE 23. *Two vertical wheels seen on Orkney. A. Wool wheel with single flyer. B. Flax wheel with two flyers.*

23

PLATE 24. *Triple flyer arrangement. The central flyer can be used alone, or the two outer flyers can be driven and used simultaneously for two-handed spinning.*

Much more rarely, wheels are seen which have three flyers. It is most unlikely that these were used to facilitate plying as is sometimes suggested, mainly because they are flax wheels and flax was not normally plyed. Another suggestion given is that the purpose of the wheel was for it to be used for either two-bobbin flax spinning or single-bobbin wool. The three flyer wheel seen in Plate no. 8 is now at Hill House in Helensburgh, but was formerly at Old Leanach Cottage, Culloden. It is unique in having all three flyers intact. In spite of some evidence of repair and replacement they very probably represent the original flyer dimensions. If this is so, then one flyer has a marginally smaller orifice and a smaller bobbin, and one of the whorls also has a deeper groove than on the other two. This does all seem to suggest that the purpose of the third flyer might well have been to allow for very much finer flax yarn, which could only be achieved by single-bobbin spinning on a flyer with a higher twist ratio. The wheel is designed so that the same driving band would fit either arrangement.

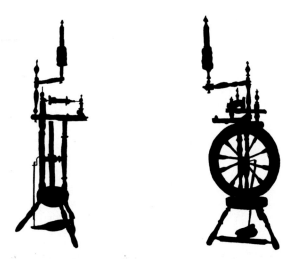

PLATE 25. *Made in 1824 by James Clement, the plan and profile views of this wheel show its great elegance. Only one of the three original flyers remains.*

24

A most beautiful privately-owned example of a three flyer wheel was made by James Clement of Crieff for the owner of the local estate of Cultoquhey. This wheel, seen in Plate no. 25, is small, delicate and elegant. Being without unnecessary ornamentation, it is made of partridge wood and finished with small ivory pegs and finials. Not only the maker's name, but also the family crest are discretely engraved on two small brass plates on the front edge of the table. Such fine examples are often called "drawing-room" wheels.

One question that remains unanswered is how the spinner managed to keep her fingers damp whilst both hands were engaged in spinning. Perhaps if the water pot was hanging below the centrally placed distaff, it would have been possible to slide the hands forward to the pot without disrupting the continuity of thread.

Castle style . . . there seems to be no reasonable explanation for this unusual construction which offers no apparent advantage to the spinner. It must be concluded that this was simply an aesthetic development. Similar wheels are found in Ireland.

PLATE 26. Two unusual styles. Above. Tall Castle wheel. Left. Wheel with Boomerang supports.

Boomerang style . . . this is specifically a wool wheel which at first sight seems to have no functional advantage in its design. It does appear, though, that if the spinner was to be seated directly in front of the flyer, it would require a well-extended right leg to reach the treadle. If, on the other hand, the spinner sat closer to the treadle than the flyer, the greater space thus created could be used for longer attenuation of her woollen thread. (See page 33 for details of spinning style.)

Wheel Makers

In 1751 an act of parliament decreed that all wheel makers should mark their name or sign upon their goods. In spite of that, most of the early wheels that still exist are unmarked. Generally the high quality "drawing room" wheels do carry an inscription which should perhaps be seen as an indication of the craftsman's own pride in his work.

During the 18th century there were literally hundreds of wheelwrights producing wheels in Scotland and it is easy to imagine that the standard, in at least some rural areas, might not always have been of the highest, and that pressure of work may have left little time for the niceties of inscribing one's name on the finished article. Take for example, the plight of John Currie a wheelwright in Ballintruim. He testified that between 1767 and 1769 he mended 487 wheels and 79 reels as well as making 20 new wheels and 28 reels. He could probably sympathise with the wheelwright in Rannoch who, at much the same time, complained that "everybody in this country by their being ignorant how to use or even spin with their wheel, put them wrong almost every day"!

Some women complained that their housing conditions were to blame for all the problems they had with their wheels, but considering the hard domestic life of the rural lower classes in those times, not much above a rugged subsistence, it is only too easy to imagine their difficulties in understanding the intricacies of this new-fangled spinning device. Like John Currie, the time of most wheelwrights must have been very largely spent in just keeping the wheels of the district "on the road".

Although the names of a number of makers of the late 18th century are recorded, almost nothing is at present known of their work. In the Country Life Archives of the National Museum of Antiquities in Edinburgh, there is some information about a few later wheel makers. For example, James Clement of Crieff, whose Cultoquhey wheel of 1824 has already been mentioned, has another wheel in the museum collection which enables a comparison to be made. It can be seen that this second wheel, although of similar design, is slightly less elegant and only bears an engraved inscription on the side of the table rather than a brass plaque.

The wheel shown in Plate no. 10 was made on the now uninhabited island of Mingulay off Barra, and we know from the Archives that it was the work of the Buchanan family who carried the tradition of wheel making into the late 1930's.

Writing about the Home Industries of the Highlands and Islands in 1912, Professor Scott reports that a Mr T. W. Anderson of Lerwick estimated that in 27 years he had sold 1,000 wheels. That represented an average of one wheel completed every ten days.

No doubt anyone wishing to follow intensive research on the subject of Scottish wheelwrights could unearth a wealth of fascinating material.

Reels and Swifts

When the wool was spun, if it had been already dyed, then it was simply wound off the bobbin or spindle into a ball ready for weaving. This was quite adequate since the carding oil would not be washed out until the weaving was complete. If the spun wool was to be washed or dyed prior to weaving, then it was necessary to make a skein. The simple method of skeining was to use a reeling stick now known as a "niddy-noddy", but in the Highlands it was formerly called a "crois iarna".

This simple length of wood had two cross pieces, one at either end, and facing in opposite directions. By winding the yarn up and down as the stick was rotated, a skein could be made that was four times the length of the stick. There was never a standard length to these sticks but 18 ins was common.

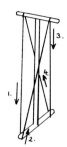

PLATE 27. Method of making a skein on a 'niddy-noddy'.

For linen yarn a more uniform measure was needed and reels became common. If a skein was of a set number of strands around a reel of standard length, then clearly the weight of that yarn would indicate its fineness. In this way it was hoped to establish standardised measurements, but there is no evidence that this was achieved. Many reels can be found with click devices which indicate when a set number of rounds have been completed. For those

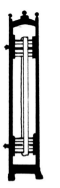

A   B

PLATE 28. A. Jack reel with counting device, for skeining flax. B. Elegant upright 'swift' with revolving 'rice' type drums.

27

who were without any counting device, a simple method was known to have been used. The person reeling off the yarn, and this was often not the spinner herself, filled a pocket with a counted number of small stones. For each revolution of the reel she dropped one stone into a bowl so that when her pocket was empty the skein was complete.

The purpose of a swift was that of unwinding a skein. If wool or flax had been skeined prior to weaving, the person winding the pirns would fix that skein over the adjustable arms of a swift which then revolved as the yarn was unwound.

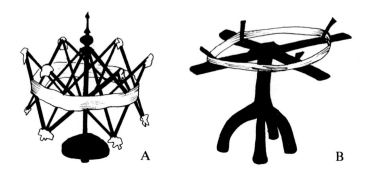

PLATE 29. A. 19th century 'drawing-room' swift, adjustable yew-wood arms on a brass column. B. Rural revolving swift made with tree trunk and planks.

Spinning Schools

The fact that spinning schools were set up by the Trustees of the Forfeited Estates has already been mentioned. Although the long-term benefit of many of these schools turned out to be negligible, the initial impact that these establishments must have had on poor rural communities can well be imagined.

The surveyor who went out to the remote North West to find sites for the first four schools reported that in these areas there was great poverty, and that the clothing of the people was scanty and worn until it was in rags. In areas such as this, 40 girls at a time were given three months' instruction, and when they could spin they were given a wheel and reel and often other small prizes such as a silk handkerchief or cap. Of course, there were those who attended the school managing to conceal the fact that they could spin already, and the odd few who were still trying to master the art after a year. Sadly it was in these areas where the help was most needed that the scheme was said to have utterly failed and was eventually abandoned. The reasons for failure are various, but the cost of transport for raw materials and finished goods, the problems of organisation in remote areas, and the inability or reluctance of traditional rural communities to become efficient and highly organised were all given as reasons.

The story was different elsewhere. The spinning school in Stornoway was said to be a great success even though they grew little flax themselves and, for want of a weaver, sent the yarn to Ireland for weaving.

In Inverness, a most successful spinning school taught 184 girls to spin in 1753. Poor girls were provided with wheels and reels and country girls were given free accommodation. But the greatest concentration of schools developed in the Southern Highlands around Callander and east of Stirling where there was already a nucleus of small textile industries able to employ the skilled spinners.

Many lairds had a patriarchal concern for the welfare of their estate workers and tenants, and some financed schools privately. They gave away wheels to their tenants, whilst those girls who could afford the 9s that it cost for a wheel and reel bought their own.

During these years, literally thousands of spinning wheels must have been made and distributed through the Highlands. In 1753 the Trustees sent 100 wheels to the estate of Cluny alone and a wheelwright was considered an essential craftsman to be settled in each community.

Whether or not spinning schools were successful in economic terms, they achieved one remarkable end. In just a few short years the new flyer spinning wheel was introduced to virtually all the inhabitants of the most remote part of Britain, namely the Highlands and Islands of Scotland.

PLATE 30. Directions of yarn twist.

𝒫ly

Today the term "ply" when associated with wool is used to denote the thickness or weight of yarn. The original meaning was to indicate the number of previously spun single threads that were then twisted together to form the final yarn. Two-ply indicates the use of two threads, three-ply of three threads etc.

Plying was not normally practiced for the weaving of linen, hard tartan or Harris tweed, but it was employed for the creation of the gossamer threads of Shetland lace knitting and for the soft Shetland and Fair Isle knitted jerseys.

Among several samples of early 18th century hard tartan from the Hebrides which are held at the Tartan Museum in Comrie, two have a fine two-ply warp. This, however, was an unusual feature of hard cloth.

𝒯wist

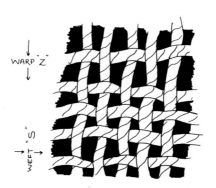

WARP "Z"

WEFT "S"

PLATE 31. Angles of twist in fabric woven from 'Z' spun warp and 'S' spun weft.

If the flyer or spindle are rotated in a clockwise direction, then the twist that is put into the yarn will also have a clockwise nature. Anti-clockwise rotation of the flyer or spindle will create an anti-clockwise twist. When looking at the twisted yarns, the angle of the line formed between twists lies at a diagonal, the direction of which can be matched to the central stroke of the letters "S" or "Z", which are in turn the names given to the yarns. "Z" twist is created when the flyer rotates clockwise, and "S" twist occurs when the rotation is anti-clockwise. Plate no. 30 shows these twists.

PLATE 32. Miss Constance Astley of Arisaig, a craft enthusiast who taught wood carving in the village, is seen demonstrating her excellent spinning skill. Probable date about 1870. (Photograph by Courtesy of Arisaig S.W.R.I., taken from their book about the village).

PLATE 33. Detail of a handspun and knitted Shetland shawl which measures 6 ft 6 ins square yet can slip through a wedding ring.

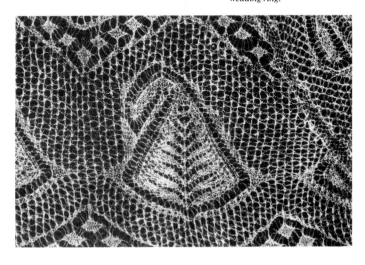

31

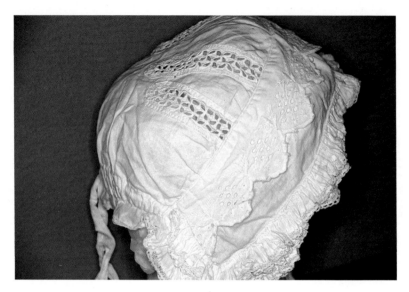

PLATE 34. A linen Mutch with applied cotton decoration. Formerly an important item of a married woman's dress. (Photographed at, and printed by Courtesy of, The Highland Folk Museum, Kingussie).

PLATE 35. Detail of a Plaide which was dyed, spun and woven by Christina Young. Dated 1726. (Photographed at, and printed by Courtesy of, The Scottish Tartans Museum, Comrie, Perthshire).

32

From the middle ages to the 17th century, "Z" spinning was preferred and believed to produce a better quality of woven cloth, and in early excavated textiles "S" spun yarns are often coarser than "Z".

It is also interesting that where cloth is made from "Z" warp and "S" weft (or the other way round) the angle of twist will be the same over the whole fabric and it has been suggested that this made it easier to obtain a "nap" or raised surface on the cloth. Plate no. 31 shows this quite clearly.

When yarns are plyed, usually for knitting purposes, it is necessary for the direction of twist used in plying to be opposite to that used for the initial singles spinning. In other words, two "Z" spun singles will be "S" plyed. If this is not done then the result will be overtwisted yarn unsuitable for either weaving or knitting.

When using a flyer wheel the spinner could rotate the wheel easily in either direction according to whether "S" or "Z" twist was required. This was not so easy on the muckle wheel and here it was normal for a twist to be put in the driving band, see Plate no. 12, so that a forward rotating wheel would reverse the direction of the spindle. When hand spindles were used, twisting by the fingers would almost always create clockwise momentum if the right hand was used. Thigh twirling with the right hand and spindle on the right thigh would cause the opposite anti-clockwise rotation of the spindle. Left-handed spinners would obviously reverse all of these directions.

Style

The one area in the whole subject of spinning that rarely receives a mention in early literature is that of the style or technique of the spinner. For example, much is written about two-handed flax wheels, but the method of dressing the distaff and drawing out the threads from it are never described.

Speaking of wool spinning and writing at the beginning of the 20th century, John Firth in Orkney was an exception. He wrote that spinning was at that time done without any affected posing, but that 60 years before "the ability of a spinner was judged largely by the dainty play of fingers and the graceful flourishes she gave as with the right hand the rowar (rolag) was gradually extended to arms length". He was describing the method that in today's craft books would be called "long draw" involving the attenuation of a rolag, which is held at either end to control the degree of twist allowed on to the extending yarn. Plate no. 32 shows Miss Constance Astley spinning at Arisaig on the west coast in the 1870's. The rolags can be seen on her lap waiting to be used, and the beginning of the attenuation of the fibres can be seen occurring between her hands. The origin of her wheel is not known, but it has the appearance of an English rather than local construction.

The Textiles

Having seen how spinning evolved and developed in Scotland and the way in which the practice of the art affected the lives of the people, it is finally desirable to look at the product of this labour, the textiles.

Plaiding

During the 17th century a great deal of woollen cloth or plaiding was made in Scotland, and much of this was exported especially through the east coast ports of Inverness and Aberdeen. Highlanders were known to trek from Fort William in the west to Inverness in the east in order to trade their woven goods. The general quality of plaiding was never very high and in spite of concerted efforts to maintain a set standard, it was the failure to achieve this that contributed most to the eventual decline of the trade. Ultimately, the Europeans decided to buy only the raw wool from Scotland and manufacture their own goods.

Coarse plaiding was always woven by the people to serve their own domestic needs, and by selling any small surplus they were able to purchase other vital commodities. In many cases, a system of direct exchange or barter with the merchants was used.

Stockings

With knitted woollens it was a different story. Throughout the 18th century the trade in knitted stockings in the Aberdeen area was outstanding, not only in terms of quality, but also quantity — Thomas Pennant reported that 69,333 dozen pairs were sold annually. At the beginning of the century the women of Aberdeen were said to have the skill to produce woollen stockings that were finer than silk, and at the end of the century the price of stockings ranged from 10s to 30s a pair. (Remember that a spinning wheel and reel at that time cost 9s.)

Many travellers reported on the great industry of the women in Aberdeen who paid for the rent of their land with the product of their handwork and made their husbands' clothes besides. Each morning the women poured in to Aberdeen with stockings to sell; indeed to meet the needs of this trade both wool and oil were specifically imported.

Weavers and Tailors

Outside of the major trade areas such as Aberdeen, women were engaged in spinning and weaving mainly to supply the needs of their families and often completing the whole process from sheep to garment in their own homes. Some communities supported a wool or linen weaver who would undertake the final making of the cloth. For those with the necessary finance to pay for their services, the travelling tailors who visited many areas could be engaged to make up the final garments. Other visitors to outlying districts included carriers and packmen who not only brought wares with them to sell but also purchased from the women any surplus yarn, cloth, or linen thread.

Bonnets

Bonnet making was another area in which woollen yarn and the skill of the knitter was employed. The blue-dyed fleece was spun and then knitted on four pins to about twice the intended size. Then it was shrunk and felted to create a waterproof finish before finally being dried on a frame.

Tartan

References are made to tartan alone and to tartan plaiding. Clan tartans as we know them today, probably did not evolve until the 19th century, but in the 17th and 18th centuries multi-coloured cloth was made by the intermingling of bands of similar colours in both warp and weft.

Few positive facts exist about the exact nature of early rural tartan. However, the Christina Young plaide, a detail of which is shown in Plate no. 35, is dated 1726 and was handspun, dyed and woven by one lady and is a most perfect example of the skills of that time. Measuring approximately 16ft by 6ft, it contains about 22 miles of handspun single-ply yarn. It is said to have taken Christina Young 8 years to complete, and was certainly not an everyday plaide but was made to be an heirloom.

Most tartan of the 18th-19th century was made in hard spun worsted yarn tightly packed in weaving. In this way no subsequent fulling of the cloth was needed, and the strong colours were not then muted by a hairy cloth surface. In the same way these bright colours would not suffer any dulling or weakening from the alkaline solutions normally used in fulling. Indeed, the cloth was probably given a final wash in an acid solution such as fresh urine, which would increase the firmness of the cloth.

True "hard tartan" was a stiff almost board-like material, that could only have been made from a long and straight fleece spun in a worsted style. To be able to withstand the tension, friction and beating that such close weaving would have required, the yarn must have been spun evenly and without fault, with sufficient twist to make it strong but not so much that it would snap under tension. To produce such yarn required great skill and the use of carefully selected fleece.

Shetland Knitting

Certainly as far back as the 16th century and possibly earlier the Shetland Isles were noted for knitting. Fishing boats from Holland made regular visits to the islands and it is suggested that knitted hose and cloth were used by the Shetlanders as a kind of international currency. Professor Scott actually considered that the idea of knitted hose had originally come to mainland Scotland from the Shetlands.

It was only towards the middle of the 19th century that the now famous arts of Fair Isle knitting and cobweb lace shawls were developed. In both cases, it was the fancy of the London fashion market that produced the demand and the outlet for these goods as well as the stimulus that was to produce some very remarkable spinning skill.

The knitting of lace was already practiced in Europe and England, but it was the introduction of cotton from India that first caused the appearance of very fine lace knitting.

By using the finest neck fleece from the native Shetland sheep, the women of these islands were able to equal the skill of the cotton spinners elsewhere. Inspiration for designs was found in the popular printed materials of the time and the Indian lozenge shape shown in Plate no. 33 would have been copied from the Paisley shawls then being made in Scotland. This particular shawl measures about 6 ft 6 ins square, yet weighs only 100g, and is fine enough to pass through a wedding ring. The yarn is two-ply and considerably finer than modern sewing thread. It was said to take 2 to 3 years to spin and knit such a shawl. On completion, the article would be carefully washed and then stretched on the ground or on a specially constructed frame, and left to dry. They were sometimes whitened by fumes in sulphur boxes.

In these islands it was usual for a special belt to be worn into which the ends of the knitting pins could be slotted. This enabled women to attend to their chores without laying down their work in much the same way as the spindle spinners two centuries earlier. Fine lace knitting required total attention, but general and Fair Isle work could be treated in this way.

The natural wool colours of the native Shetland sheep (namely moorit — a ginger brown, dark moorit, grey, blue-black, black and white) were used together with some home-dyed yarns, for making the complex patterns of the soft but hard wearing jerseys and mitts. A handspun two-ply yarn was used which was much fluffier than the hard worsted weaving yarns.

Tweed

The name "tweed" was at first applied to the woollen cloth produced in the Border region of Scotland. Production in that area was always run on an industrialised basis, with centralised weaving but home spinners supplying the yarn. The decline in linen production by the beginning of the 19th century concentrated resources into the wool trade once more.

It was a combination of high grade wool, attractive design and colour, durability and fine texture that eventually took Border tweed out of the hands of the traditional craftsman and rapidly into the era of mechanisation.

In the Hebrides, Harris tweed was built on a different foundation. For centuries, domestic weaving of hand-spun yarn into serviceable plaiding had been established in the islands. It took the energy and far sight of the Countess of Dunmore, wife of the new owner of Harris, to establish in 1834 the embryo of this industry. It was her vision of co-ordinating the work of individual craftsmen, sending girls away for training and of finding markets for the cloth in the cities of Scotland and England, that established an industry that is still surviving, albeit with many changes, a century and a half later.

The women spinners of the islands made use of native coarse fleece and local dyes for the production of a tough, coloured, single-ply weaving yarn. This in turn produced a waterproof, warm and hardwearing cloth much favoured by fashionable sportsmen and country folk. The women produced the dyed and spun yarns alongside their other domestic duties as a matter of economic necessity.

On the island of St Kilda, it was the decline of trade in sea-bird products that necessitated the production of tweed and blankets in the late 19th century, but this work had to be slotted into their hard life-style. In summer the sheep were caught and plucked, in early winter the yarn was spun so that the days of the long winter could be utilised for weaving. In spring the cloth was fulled or "waulked" and was ready to leave on the summer ships.

Tweed, like tartan, has become a "national product" of Scotland. The reputation of high quality that these products enjoy today was first established 150 years ago and was based on the skills of the handspinners and weavers of the time.

ℒinen

In spite of the intensity with which linen spinning and weaving occurred during the 17th and 18th centuries, few remaining samples are to be found. There are two probable reasons for this. Firstly, much of the cloth produced, particularly in the Highlands, was of poor quality and it was either exported as low grade cloth or "worn to rags" by the people themselves. Secondly, much of the flax spinning was only ever intended to produce linen thread for sewing purposes. Incredibly this also included much of the work done by the fine country ladies with their elegant "drawing room" wheels who found the production of linen thread an acceptable way of supplementing their income.

That some very fine linen spinning was carried out is not doubted, but since this yarn was usually sent to the local weaver to be made into sheets and pillow-cases, tablecloths and napkins, once again it was largely used until it was worn out and therefore few samples remain. A small collection of linen, including some fine handspun examples, is held at the Folk Museum in Kingussie. The late 18th century mutch (or kertch) shown in Plate no. 34 came from Rosemarkie in Ross and Cromarty. The base fabric is a strong but quite coarse linen and the decoration takes the form of strips of cotton lace either inlaid or applied to the base fabric. Although headresses such as this were a most important item of a married woman's dress, during the 19th century they were commonly made from cotton rather than linen material.

Dr Grant, in her book "Highland Folkways", recorded the use of linen during the 19th century for the knitting of lace stockings, although cotton again became more normal for this task. Linen was also used as a warp thread for the weaving of drugget (a coarse striped cloth used for women's skirts and aprons), the weft threads being wool. This type of cloth construction was usually called "linsey-wolsey".

Conclusion

The last commercial handspinners in Scotland were the ladies of the Outer Hebrides engaged in the production of Harris Tweed. During this present century the practice has slowly declined and it might have seemed that the art was facing its final eclipse. But then the era of the "craft" spinner arrived. It seems strange that this pastime has not received quite the same degree of enthusiastic support in Scotland with all its great spinning traditions, that it has in England, America or New Zealand, for example. However, the number of handspinners in Scotland is ever increasing and once more the art of the wheelwright is returning. Requirements for a wheel are perhaps different now but the basic designs and principles established 200 years ago remain the same.

It was upon the art of the spinner that the mighty industrial revolution was founded. Now as we reject many of the principles that mechanisation has brought into our lives, we are able to turn back to the humble spinning wheel for pleasure and relaxation. The wheel, it seems, has turned full circle.

Bibliography

Baines P. "Spinning Wheel, Spinners and Spinning" Batsford. 1977.

Born. "Spinning Wheels" Ciba Review no. 28.

Buchanan D. "Reflections of the Isle of Barra". Sands & Co. Ltd. 1942.

Buchanan M. "St. Kilda a Photographic Album" Blackwood. Edin. 1983.

Chadwick E. "The Craft of Handspinning" Batsford 1980.

Chambers Encyclopedia. 1895.

Cregeen E. R. (Ed) "Argyll Estate Instructions 1771-1805. Scottish History Soc. 1964.

Dean I. F. M. "Scottish Spinning Schools" London 1930.

Don S. "Fair Isle Knitting" Mills and Boon. 1979.

Don S. "Shetland Lace" Mills and Boon. 1980.

Dunbar. J. Telfer "The Costume of Scotland" Batsford Ltd. 1981.

Firth J. "Reminiscences of an Orkney Parish" Orkney Nat. Hist. Soc., Stromness. 1974.

Graham H. G. "Social Life of Scotland in the Eighteenth Century" London 1937.

Grant I. F. "Highland Folkways" Routledge Kegan and Paul 1961.

Gulvin C. "The Tweed Makers 1600-1914" David and Charles 1973.

Henshall A. S. "Clothing Found at Huntsgarth Harray Orkney". Proceedings from Soc. of Antiq. of Scotland. 1968-69.

Hume Brown P. "Scotland before 1700" Edin. 1893.

Hume Brown P. (Ed.) "Early Travellers in Scotland" Modern Edn. Mercat Press 1978.

Innes. C. (Ed) "Black Book of Taymouth" Bannatyne Club 1855.

Iredale J. "Preparation of Wools" in "The Wool Industry of Great Britain" ed. Jenkins.

Johnson & Boswell "Journey to the Western Islands of Scotland, and Journal of a Tour to the Hebrides with Samuel Johnson" 1775. Modern Edn. Oxford Univ. Press. 1970.

Latour A. "The Stocking" Ciba Review no. 106.

McIain R. R. "Highlanders at Home" Ackerman & Co. 1848.

Mackintosh J. "History of Civilisation in Scotland" Brown & Co. Aberdeen 1884/1888.

McKay M. (Ed.) "The Rev. Dr. John Walker's Report on the Hebrides of 1764 & 1777." John Donald Pub. Ltd. 1980.

Markham G. "A Way to get Wealth" 1676.

Martin Martin. "A Description of the Western Islands of Scotland" 2nd Edn. James Thin 1981.

Mercer J. "The Spinners Workshop" Prism Press. 1978.

Millar A. H. (Ed) "Scottish Forfeited Estate Papers" Scottish Hist. Soc. vol LV11. 1909.

Mitchell L. "Irish Spinning Dyeing and Weaving" Dundalgan Press 1978.

Munro Sir D. "Description of the Western Isles of Scotland, called Hybrides" Glasgow 1884.

Maxwell S. "Highland Dress and Tartan in the Ross of Pitcalnie Papers" Journal of the Costume Society no. 10 1976.

Pennant T. "A Tour of Scotland in 1769" Modern Edn. Melven Press 1979.

Penny G. "Traditions of Perth" Perth 1836.

Ross A. "Scottish Home Industries" 1895. Modern Edn. Molendinar Press 1976.

Ross M. "The Essentials of Handspinning" Spinningdale, Crook of Devon, Perthshire. 1980.

Ross M. "The Essentials of Yarn Design for Handspinners" Spinningdale, Crook of Devon, Perthshire. 1983.

Ryder M. L. "Sheep and Man" Duckworth. 1983.

Ryder M. L. "Sheep and Wool for Handcraft Workers" 23 Swanston Place, Edinburgh. 1978.

Ryder M. L. "The Evolution of Scottish Breeds of Sheep" Scottish Studies 12.

"Soay Sheep" leaflet pub. by the Rare Breeds Survival Trust.

Scott W. R. "Report on the Home Industries in the Highlands and Islands" Neill & Co. Ltd. 1914.

"Scottish Woollens" Nat. Assoc. of Scot. Woollen Manufacturers. 1956.

Shaw F. J. "The Northern and Western Islands of Scotland" John Donald. 1980.

Smith J. "Memoirs of Wool" London 1767. Re-published Gregg Int. Pub. Ltd. 1968.

Smout T. C. "Scottish Trade on the Eve of Union 1660-1707" Edin. 1963.

Spreull J. "Accompt Current Betwixt Scotland and England" Edin. 1705.

Teal P. "Hand Woolcombing and Spinning" Blandford Press 1976.

Thompson F. "Harris Tweed" David and Charles 1969.

Turner K. "The Legacy of the Great Wheel" Select Books Missouri 65548. 1980.

Ulster Museum "Spinning Wheels" pub. no. 168. 1976.

Walton P. "The Textiles" in Ellison and Harbottle "Excavation of a 17th Century Bastion in Newcatle upon Tyne" Archaeologia Aeliana 5th series Vol. x1 1983.

Warden A. J. "The Linen Trade" 1864.

NAMES FOR THE PARTS OF A SPINNING WHEEL

1. Legs (normally 3, but sometimes 4)
2. Table or stock.
3. Well for water bowl.
4. Mother-of-all.
5. Tension adjustment screw.
6. Orifice.
7. Distaff arm.
8. Dressed distaff.
9. Leather bearing (to support Flyer).
10. Flyer.
11. Bobbin.
12. Maiden.
13. Drive-band.
14. Wheel hub.
15. Wheel spokes.
16. Wheel.
17. Wheel uprights.
18. Footman.
19. Treadle with front bar.

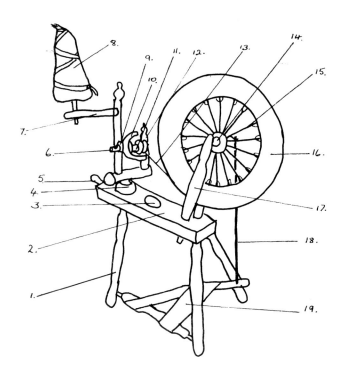

Acknowledgment

In the last few years many people have allowed me to examine their spinning wheels and tools, and have generously passed on their knowledge. I am most grateful to them all. For allowing me access to the wheels illustrated and photographed in this book I particularly thank Heather Anderson (plate 16), Ina Lowe (plate 27B), Morag MacPherson (plates 10 and 21), Mrs L. Davidson (plate 23A), Messrs Walter S. Beaton, Antique Dealers, Perth (plate 25).

At the following museums I have been given generous assistance: The Museum of Scottish Tartans, Comrie; The Highland Folk Museum, Kingussie; The Museum of Antiquities Country Life Section, Edinburgh.

Hill House, Helensburgh, and Tankerness House Museum, Kirkwall, have helped me to obtain photographs. I thank Vivienne Peck for bringing to my attention the wheel at Hill House. The staff of Sandeman Library, Perth, have found for me much useful literature for which I am indebted.

I am particularly grateful to Dorothy Dickie, Peter MacDonald and Sandy Grierson for reading the text and making many helpful suggestions, and to Mabel Ross for much advice on publishing.